ORIGINAL DAO DE JING

THE HIDDEN WAY TO SUCCESS, FREEDOM, AND ETERNITY

Laozi

Translated by Dr. Jinchun Ye

Second Edition

ISBN: 978-1-7348621-7-1 (Paperback)
ISBN: 978-1-7348621-0-2 (eBook)

Second Edition, Sept. 2022
Jin Publishing, Northbrook, USA

author@dao2win.com
https//www.dao2win.com

Preface

Dao De Jing is the Chinese classic written by Laozi (also known as Lao-Tzu or Lao-Tze, born in 604 BC, date of death unknown). The name "Laozi" is a Chinese honorary title meaning Old Master. Despite Laozi being a well-known name, he remains an obscure figure. The primary source about him is a short description in the book titled the Historical Records by Sima Qian (145 or 135 – 86 BC). The following excerpt comes from that book:

> Laozi was a person born in Quren community of Li village, Ku county, Chu state[1]. His last name is Li, first name Er, and literary name Dan. He was the official in charge of the imperial library of the Zhou dynasty.
> Confucius[2] (551 – 479 BC) went to the capital of the Zhou dynasty to ask Laozi

1. The ancient Quren community is now located in Luyi county, Henan province.
2. He is the founder of Confucianism, which focuses on etiquette to maintain the social hierarchy. Note that Laozi opposed etiquette as shown in Chapter 1—etiquette is the head of corruption. Confucianism had been the sole dynasty-supported ideology in China from the Han dynasty in 141 BC, till the end of the last dynasty around 1912 AD. The dynasties during this period were doomed. Indeed, Confucianism was the head of corruption of these dynasties.

about the knowledge of etiquette. Laozi said:
"For what you are asking for, its advocates
have rotten, and their bones as well. Only
their slogans remain. Moreover, gentlemen
who succeed keep their momentum going,
and gentlemen during a gloomy period live
with slovenliness and tiredness. I heard that
wealthy people hide their wealth to look like
they have nothing, and the appearance of
gentlemen with deep virtue looks foolish.
Remove your pride and excessive desires,
bright appearance, and wild wills as well.
None of these benefit you. That is all I can
tell you." Confucius left and told his stu-
dents: "Birds I know can fly; fish I know can
swim; animals I know can walk. Those who
walk can be hunted by nets; those who swim
can be hunted by fishing threads; those who
fly can be hunted by arrows. Yet, for drag-
ons, I do not know they fly with the wind
and clouds to heaven. I saw Laozi today; he
is like a dragon."

Laozi cultivated the Dao and virtue[3] and
was engaged in self-hiddenness and being
unknown[4]. Laozi had lived in the capital of

---

3. Laozi cultivated virtue through meditation and right life altitude to get the
   Dao since the Dao does not need to be developed (see the discussion of the
   Dao and virtue in the last paragraphs of the preface). As Laozi had the Dao,
   he was a saint who had all-encompassing and true knowledge.
4. This statement shall be understood as the hiddenness and no desire to be
   great on the mental level as Laozi worked until his 80s (see the next footnote) and was a well-known person in his time as well.

the Zhou dynasty for a long time. He saw the decline of the Zhou dynasty and then left[5]. When he arrived at the Hangu garrison, the garrison officer Yin Xi said: "You will retire. Please write a book for me." Then, Laozi wrote a two-part book of over five thousand words, which discussed the Dao and virtue. After that, no one knew where he went.

The book has two parts. One part is called 'Dao Jing' (i.e., the canon of the Dao), and the other 'De Jing' (i.e., the canon of virtue). It is called 'Dao De Jing'. The book written by Laozi around 520 BC (see footnote 5) became a vital scripture in Chinese literature. Since its debut, many individuals, including emperors, scholars, and school founders, have edited and annotated the manuscript. Alas, edited words are arbitrary.

There are numerous versions of Laozi's book, but the original is lost. The following will provide an overview of the popular versions and recently found ancient versions of Laozi's manuscript. Then, rationales will be presented to determine the Chinese version that is best to understand Laozi's ideas. The popular versions are the following:

---

5. The departure of Laozi happened no later than 516 BC when the Zhou dynasty lost its archives. Meanwhile, it should be after the meeting with Confucius around 523 BC. Thus, Laozi left the Zhou dynasty sometime between about 523 BC and 516 BC. During this time, Laozi was about 82- to 89-year-old. Therefore, Laozi's retirement is not due to the decline of the Zhou dynasty, and it had continued for a prolonged time before his retirement.

- Wang Bi version: Annotated and edited by Bi Wang (226 – 249 AD). This is the most popular version.
- Heshang Gong version: Annotated and edited by Heshang Gong during the reign of Emperor Wen of the Han dynasty (180 – 157 BC).
- Fu Yi ancient version: Annotated and edited by the scholar Yi Fu (555 – 639 AD). Yi Fu got the original manuscript. However, he combined other versions to form his.
- Yan Zun version: Annotated and edited by Zun Yan (about 80 BC – 10 AD). Only De Jing is available.

Note that the popular versions put 'Dao Jing' as Part I and 'De Jing' as Part II.

Of late, four ancient versions of the text were discovered as discussed below:

- Guodian Chu Slips (GCS): Unearthed in 1993 from a tomb in Guodian village in Jingmen, Hubei province. These slips were dated to around 300 BC and included about two-fifths of Laozi's text. These were excerpts the collector deemed valuable. The strips are disorganized and have no consistency.
- Peking University Han Bamboo Strips (PUHBS): In 2009, Peking University received a donation of about 3300 Bamboo Strips dated back to the Han dynasty. These strips include an almost complete version of Laozi's

text. According to the traditional Chinese naming taboo to avoid imperial first names, this version avoids using the Chinese character that is the first name of Emperor Gaozu (the founding emperor of the Han dynasty, reigning from 202-195 BC). Meanwhile, it contains the character of the first name of Emperor Hui of the Han dynasty (the second emperor of Han, reigning from 195 – 188 BC). Therefore, it must have been written during the reigning period of Emperor Gaozu, that is, 202-195 BC.

- Mawangdui Silk Texts: In 1973, copies of early Chinese books, known as Mawangdui[6] Silk Texts, were discovered in a tomb dated to 168 BC. They include two copies of Laozi's book. One copy uses older Chinese characters. Researchers call the tome with the older characters Silk Text A, and the other Silk Text B. Further, Silk Text A contains the Chinese character of the first name of Emperor Gaozu of the Han dynasty, reigning between 202 BC and 195 BC. Therefore, according to the taboo again, Silk Text A must have been written before 202 BC. Likewise, Silk Text B avoids using the character of the first name of Emperor Gaozu. Meanwhile, it contains the character of the first name of Emperor Hui of

---

6. Mawangdui is an archeological site in the east suburb of Changsha, the capital of Hunan province, China.

the Han dynasty, reigning between 195 BC and 188 BC. Thus, Silk Text B must have been written between 202 BC and 195 BC.

However, we cannot determine which one is the oldest. First of all, Dao De Jing was written about 520 BC. So, the GCS was completed between about 520 BC and about 300 BC, and Silk Text A between about 520 BC and 202 BC. Both ranges overlap significantly. Therefore, which one is older cannot be determined[7]. Meanwhile, it is clear that both versions were written ahead of the others. After that, Silk Text B and the PUHBS came next as they were written between 202 BC and 195 BC. Also, these four versions are older than the popular versions. One important difference between the ancient and popular versions is the reverse order of two parts, that is, 'De Jing' is Part I, and 'Dao Jing' is Part II.

Now, two questions arise. Are these ancient versions better? Which version is the best? As we examine the contents, both the GCS and the PUHBS are similar to the popular versions, but the Silk Texts differ from the popular versions. Following is an obvious example:

Version	Sentence
Silk Text A	Missing due to damage
Silk Text B	Supreme talent is exempted from completion (see Chapter 3).

---

7. It is a 65% chance that the GCS is older than Silk Text A, while a 35% chance that Silk Text A is older than the GCS.

GCS	Supreme talent is completed slowly.
PUHBS	Supreme talent is completed slowly.
Popular versions	Supreme talent is completed lately.

Based on the table above, the meanings of the sentences in the GCS and the PUHBS are close to the ones in the popular versions, while the meaning of the sentence in Silk Text B is completely different. Exemption from completion is consistent with non-action, so the sentence in Silk Text B conveys the Laozi's true meaning.

The GCS, one of the two oldest, suffered severe defects. First, it has two-fifths of the manuscript. It is the excerpts from the complete text. Second, it is disorganized and has no consistency. Third, the book has been edited. Thus, the GCS is not original.

Both Silk Texts are much different from the popular versions in terms of characters. Numerous cases show that they reflect accurately what Laozi wanted to convey during the journey of discovering Laozi's true wisdom. Let us discuss two inspiring examples as follows:

- Silk Text B has the sentence—saints always have no hidden possessions in their hearts and take the hearts after hundreds of introspections as their hearts (see Chapter 12), and the other versions (except Silk Text A due to missing a key Chinese character with the meaning of introspection) have the

corresponding sentences—saints always
have no heart and take the ordinary people's
hearts as their hearts. Clearly, the sentence in
Silk Text B states that saints remove possessions from their mental fields by hundreds
of introspections. However, the sentences in
the other versions are confusing; what are
the hearts of ordinary people? Some people
have wicked hearts; some have good hearts.
What are they talking about? For this sentence in Silk Text A, the key Chinese word
with the meaning of introspection is missing
due to damage. Yet, another sentence in Silk
Text A—Dao's messengers (i.e., saints) are
not benevolent in that they take hundreds of
introspections as the sheepdog (see Chapter
53)—expresses a similar meaning, that is,
Dao's messengers do not have their prejudices but follow the Dao who is the supreme
guide after hundreds of introspections. On
the other hand, the corresponding sentences
in the other versions including Silk Text B—
saints are not benevolent in that they treat
ordinary people as straw dogs—depict that
saints are unreasonably cold-hearted.

- Silk Text A has the sentence—five colors
  make people's eyes bright (see Chapter 60),
  and the other versions including Silk Text B
  have the corresponding sentences—five colors make people blind. Which one did Laozi
  intend to say? Let us ponder... People look

for desirable things due to their bright eyes, as discussed in the chapter. Hence, bright eyes are the first to cause desires. That is why Laozi used the word 'therefore' to show the logical connection in the context and suggested the saint's management is not for eyes.

The above two examples are delicate and subject to be edited, the second one in particular. They show that Silk Text A has internal consistency and no trace of being edited. Silk Text B was lightly edited, but it is better than the others except for Silk Text A. Since both Silk Texts eroded over time, the following rules create the Chinese base text. First, Silk Text A is used as the base. If Chinese characters are missing, then Silk Text B complements it. This way, the text is almost complete and has about 170 characters missing, for which suitable ones from other versions are selected in terms of internal consistency. If the residue of a character in Silk Text A cannot determine the character but indicates a different character from the other versions, then that character is omitted.

The Silk Texts are from the book, 'Mawangdui Han Tomb Silk Text (Part I)', edited by The Research Chamber of Ancient Literature, State Administration of Cultural Heritage, China. It was published by Cultural Relics Publishing House in 1980. It is the authoritative source for accessing the Silk Texts. Notably, similar rules as above form a combined text in that book too. However, that text is still impacted, for example, characters from the popular versions often replace the characters in the Silk Texts, while the Chinese base version created for translation uses the characters in the Silk Texts whenever they are available with no editing.

Understanding such an old version of Laozi's book is challenging as the meaning of a Chinese character has gone through a lot of development. The meaning may not have been the same twenty-five hundred years ago. In addition, the meanings of some ancient characters remain unknown. Thus, such an old book is written in a foreign language for the contemporary Chinese generation. Nowadays, it is easy to access a list of meanings for a character. However, someone determines the correct meaning. Below are pointers on how to understand characters in the text and the text itself. For these purposes, the original meanings[8] of characters and the internal consistency of the text provide guidance. There are two aspects of internal consistency. One is the logic within a chapter. The text uses many logical connectors, like 'hence, 'so', 'therefore', and so on. These logical connectors help determine the meanings of characters in the context. The other aspect is the connections of sentences in different chapters. The interpretations need to be consistent. Thus, those

---

8. The original meanings of characters may be more appropriate for such an old text. They can be known by the components of characters or by ancient dictionaries, for example, Shuowen Jiezi, by Xu Shen (58 – 148 AD).

sentences are annotated in assorted paragraphs to form the book into an organic whole.

Throughout the journey to understand Laozi, the existing interpretations of Laozi's book were the biggest obstacle since those specious views limited new and rational perspectives. As these stereotypes waned, the new, reasonable, and easy-to-understand Laozi's wisdom came to life. The new wisdom is no longer confusing; it is no longer empty preaching. Instead, it reveals the hidden way to success, freedom, and eternity; it gives us strength and courage; it is universal and timeless, so it is useful to all lives from ancient times to today.

Last, let us discuss the two fundamentals of the book: Dao and De. What does Dao mean? Laozi most often used the Chinese character whose pinyin is Dao to call the supreme being found by him. According to the book, the Dao is the mother of heaven and earth. Hence, the Dao is often called the Mother and the Woman. Besides, several aliases for the Dao are used:

- The Incomparable (see Chapters 1, 19, 27, 40, 60, and 67): The Dao is unable to be compared and thus unnamable.
- Sun (see Chapter 4): The Dao resembles the sun in warmth and brilliance.
- The knowing one (see Chapter 21): The Dao is living and knows all under heaven.
- I (see Chapters 37 and 83): The Dao is our true self after we abandon our possessions. The true I am great and all-knowing.

- Gem/Key within (see Chapter 37 and Chapter 53): The Dao is our guide since only the Dao is good at initiation and accomplishment.
- The God of the Creek (see Chapter 54): The Dao pours the Water whose use is endless.

The Dao is unnamable and thus cannot be grasped by the human mind, but she is the only one who is good at initiation and accomplishment. We should hold her to handle tasks and succeed, including managing a country. This leads to the next topic.

About De, it denotes virtue. People often believe that virtue is equal to adhering to a set of moral principles. The first sentence of the book indicate that upper virtue cannot be defined by ethics. Instead, Laozi introduced the revolutionary definition (De), i.e., upper virtue is nonaction. Note that nonaction is free of intended and dependent actions, so it can be reached with no possessions. Most of us think our possessions are indispensable to our existence, but Laozi realized that we are imprisoned by objects because of our possessions. Furthermore, we are no longer limited by objects without possessions; we will connect to the Dao who is the supreme guide. Note that possessions are on the mental level, like learned knowledge, the influence of our families and societies, our experience, etc., and become part of our life. To free ourselves from possessions, the entrance point is to correct our knowledge with the help of the book. With the right mindset as discussed briefly in the next paragraph, we will act correctly to get help from the Dao, and then we will enter the hidden way to success, freedom, and eternity.

The Dao's help transpires through what she pours, which is called the Water (also called Oneness, Words, etc.). To get her help, we need to get and accumulate the Water. To this purpose, caution and inspection are the two essential attitudes to detect and resolve any things and issues that block the Water. Then, how do we put the Water in use? If we humble ourselves and are kind in our daily life, then the Water will serve us best for all aspects of our life (see Chapter 56). Along this line, the Laozi's definition of upper virtue as nonaction is clear as upper virtue comes from the unlimited abilities of the Water.

PART I:

CANON OF VIRTUE (DE JING)

1

People of upper virtue have no virtue[1], so they have virtue. People of inferior virtue do not want to lose virtue, so they have no virtue. People of upper virtue have nonaction[2] and so no dependent action. People of upper benevolence act for purposes but have no dependent action. People of upper righteousness act for purposes, and the actions conform to knowledge. People of upper etiquette act for purposes, and, if they do not get a response, they will roll up their sleeves and get angry. So, the Dao[3] is lost[4]. After the Dao is lost, there comes virtue. After virtue is lost, there comes benevolence. After benevolence is lost, there comes righteousness. After righteousness is lost, there comes etiquette. Etiquette is the shallowness of fidelity and trust; it is the head of

---

1. Virtue here refers to conformity of one's life and conduct to moral and ethical principles.
2. Nonaction refers to no actions with purposes. It is the supreme state of existence without possessions. According to Chapter 6, we are no longer limited by objects in the state of nonaction.
3. The Dao is the supreme being found by Laozi. The Dao is the mother of heaven and earth and is female (see Chapter 54 to call the Dao the hidden and distant female). She is unnamable and is like the gem within. See the description of the Dao in Chapter 71.
4. At the beginning, we were with the Dao. Knowledge caused us to separate from her (see Chapter 18).

corruption. The past cognition is Dao's flowers; it is
the head of stupidity. Therefore, a great man dwells
on the depth[5] but not on the shallowness; he dwells
on her effect[6] but not on her flowers. Hence, we shall
remove the surface to get the Incomparable[7].

---

5. The depth refers to the deep fidelity and trust.
6. Only the Dao is good at initiation and accomplishment (see Chapter 3).
7. The Incomparable refers to the Dao (see Chapters 19, 27, 40, 60, and 67 as
   well). The Dao is unable to be compared and thus unnamable. So, remove
   the past cognition, i.e., knowledge, for comparison to get the Dao.

2

About those who subdue themselves to obtain Oneness[1]: Heaven obtained Oneness to be clear; earth obtained Oneness to be steady; gods obtained Oneness to be effective; the Creek[2] obtained Oneness to be full; kings[3] obtained Oneness to take it as the standard. Oneness causes these phenomena. If heaven does not stop to be clear, it would be blocked. If earth does not stop to be steady, it would produce earthquakes. If gods do not stop to be effective, they would rest. If the Creek does not stop to be full to guide all under heaven, it would be thirsty. If kings do not stop to be noble and thus high, there would be disobedience. Hence, one will certainly be noble if humility is the essence of his/her manners; one will certainly be exalted if lowliness is the foundation of his/her manners.

---

1. Oneness is produced by the Dao (the Dao's Words / Water). It is unnamable, almost identical to the Dao. Its use is supreme and unexhausted, as described in this chapter. Part II, 'Canon of Dao', discusses Oneness extensively (see Chapters 52, 54, 56, 81, etc.).
2. The Creek refers to what the Dao streams (see Chapter 52 and Chapter 54). It can manage all under heaven for a lot of great things if the Dao is under heaven (see Chapter 78 and Chapter 81).
3. Note that we need to understand a king is a ruler but do not distinguish the gender.

Therefore, kings identify as orphaned, widowed, and childless. Essences result from such humility[4], don't they? Hence, one with innumerable companions is companionless. Therefore, we should not desire to be favorable like gems nor bothersome like stones.

---

4. This is because the Water (i.e., Oneness) stays in the places that are disliked by the multitude according to Chapter 56.

3

After superior people hear the Dao, few can walk with her[1]; when mediocre people hear the Dao, they doubt her existence; when inferior people hear the Dao, they mock her. If she had not been mocked, she wouldn't have been the Dao. Therefore, the suggestions to have her are provided: "Uncovering the Dao follows the expenditure. Entering the Dao follows the retreat[2]. Pleasing the Dao follows similarity[3]. The upper virtue follows the act of cleansing oneself. The supreme brilliance follows endurance. The virtue of open-mindedness follows the act of not being full[4]. The virtue of creativity follows the act of emptying. The transformation of character to ascend to heaven follows soilage[5]. The supreme union has no companion[6]. The supreme talent is

---

1. Even though superior people believe in the existence of the Dao, they still need the right guidance as provided in this chapter to get her.
2. Retreat: the act of withdrawing into privacy.
3. Similarity: the act of not differencing.
4. According to Chapter 40, the act of not being full is embodied in the act of not being self-opinioned and not being arrogant.
5. As one does not care about appearance to follow others to pursue goods, he/she will transform and return to the unlimited state (see Chapter 74).
6. A similar statement in Chapter 2—one with innumerable companions is companionless.

exempted from completion. The supreme sound is almost inaudible[7]. The heavenly image has no punishment[8]. The Dao is like the gem within clothing and is unnamable. Only the Dao is good at initiation and accomplishment."

---

7. The supreme sound refers to the words outgoing from the Dao (see Chapter 81).
8. See Chapter 81 for the details.

4

Toward a forbearing one does the Dao move; toward a weak one does the Dao apply her use. Objects under heaven are born from possessions[1]; possessions are born from emptiness[2]. The Dao produces Oneness; Oneness produces earth; earth produces laws of heaven, earth, and people; the laws produce all objects. All objects carry darkness[3] and embrace the sun[4]; air[5] between coordinates them.

---

1. In this book, possessions shall be understood as what we have mentally from the past cognition. While we usually take our possessions as treasure, we are confined under heaven and distinctive, self-opinionated, reactive, etc., because of our possessions.
2. Emptiness is the passage to Oneness. In other words, possessions are the blockage to Oneness.
3. Darkness refers to possessions according to the context.
4. Sun: something resembling the sun in warmth or brilliance. Here, it refers to the Dao according to the context.
5. According to the context, air refers to Oneness.

5

The most abhorrent thing under heaven is to be orphaned, widowed, and childless. However, kings identify as such. Do not believe that harm is beneficial to children[1] and benefaction causes harm[2]. Thus, for human teachings, discuss them at night to teach[3]. Hence, anyone who forces children to be excellent needs to be doomed. I will take it as the rule of study.

---

1. Laozi opposed harsh ways of teaching and parenting. Instead, he emphasized the importance of children's mental wellness.
2. This sentence clearly supports encouragement in education and opposes use of violence in education.
3. Discussion at night is informal and not forcible.

6

One under heaven who reaches softness[1] travels swiftly among the hardest under heaven. One without possession crosses the solid matter. Thereby, one who is limited under heaven knows the benefits of nonaction. For nonverbal guidance[2] and the benefits of nonaction, nothing can be comparable to them under heaven.

1. See Chapter 58 for how to reach softness.
2. It refers to leading by example and also appears in Chapter 50.

7

Which one is dearer, a name or life? Which one is more precious, life or goods? Which one is sickness, acquirement or loss? One must pay a high cost for what is beloved and suffer a big loss for a large collection. Hence, one with the awareness of being lowly is not disgraced; one with the awareness of refrainment does not have dangers and can have a long life[1].

---

1. A similar statement in Chapter 78.

8

The supreme being seems absent[1]; her use is invaluable. The supreme full seems streaming[2]; its use is unlimited. Superior understanding follows inquiries[3]; superior ingenuity follows solid work; superior wins follow illumination[4]. Haste is better than coldness[5]; attraction[6] is better than distinction. Invitation and attraction can be the norm under heaven.

1. The supreme being refers to the Dao, and she is always unnamable (see Chapter 78 and Chapter 83).
2. The supreme full refers to what the Dao streams (see Chapter 52).
3. So, do not jump to conclusions.
4. Illumination is described in Chapters 17, 20, 64, 68, 69, 73, 79, and 82..
5. Cold: not friendly, unresponsive. Coldness is worst since haste is depreciated as well (see Chapter 72).
6. The lowly manner is the key to attraction (see Chapter 26).

❧❧❧❧❧❧❧　**9**　❧❧❧❧❧❧❧

If a kingdom has the Dao, transporting horses retire to futility. If a kingdom does not have the Dao, battle horses are born in its vicinity.

10

No sin[1] is greater than indulgence; no disaster is greater than not knowing to be lowly; no fault is more painful than the desire of possessing. Hence, sufficiency growing from the awareness of being lowly is permanent sufficiency. One can know all under heaven without leaving his/her house and know divine laws without observance through windows. If one travels farther, his/her knowledge becomes more limited. Therefore, saints[2] know all under heaven without traveling, give names without seeing, and succeed without actions.

---

1. The original meaning of sin in Chinese is a net that captures malevolent people. As indicated in Chapter 60, those desirable things trap people so they cannot hear from the Dao.
2. A saint refers to a person who connects to the Dao, so he/she is all-knowing.

11

One who engages in study increases actions daily. One after hearing the Dao reduces actions daily; he/she reduces them until nonaction; he/she has no dependent actions as well due to nonaction. Desiring to acquire all under heaven, one shall have no issues always. One with issues cannot acquire all under heaven.

~~~~~~~~~~ **12** ~~~~~~~~~~

Saints always have no hidden possessions in their hearts[1] and take the hearts after hundreds of intro-spections[2] as their hearts. Both mild and hostile people are benign to the saints because kindness is their nature. Both trusting and skeptical people trust them because trustfulness is their nature. For various voices in their dominions, saints are keen to restrain their hearts as they rule. People link to their eyes and ears; saints smile on all of them[3].

---

1. A heart is a mental field where possessions hide. An ideal heart is deep and clear, and there are no possessions in it.
2. The phrase, hundreds of introspections, also appears in Chapter 53 and Chapter 65.
3. Saints do not react to what they hear and see.

13

From birth to death, people who belong to life are about three out of ten; people who belong to death are about three out of ten. However, people live in the name of living[1], but all their movements create dead spots; these people are about three out of ten. Why? Because they live for life[2]. I hear that some people are good at holding life[3]. They do not avoid arrows and tigers during travel in mountains; they do not wear armor in battle. They have no place for tips of arrows to pierce through, for tigers to put claws on, and for blades of weapons to slash. Why? Because they have no dead spots.

---

1. Live: to continue to have a physical life.
2. In other words, they pursue longevity.
3. The Dao is life. Non-Dao means death (see Chapter 20 and Chapter 76).

14

The Dao bears us[1]; virtue raises us[2]. Objects restrict us; we become instruments. Hence, myriad objects respect the Dao and value virtue. The Dao is respectful and virtue is precious because they do not set up a hierarchy but let the objects be themselves always.

---

1. The pronoun 'us' refers to the set of all 'I's according to the context. In other words, it refers to the souls of all objects. This sentence is repeated in the next chapter and Chapter 58.
2. Note that virtue is not the act of adhering to ethics. Instead, virtue refers to the act of holding the Dao as it is the Dao who raises us (see the next chapter).

~~~~~~~~~~ **15** ~~~~~~~~~~

</div>

The Dao bears us, raises us, grows us, fulfills us, settles us, [...][1] us, sustains us, and returns us. She gives birth but does not have the act of owning[2]; she serves but does not set up an administration; she promotes growth but does not have the act of slaughtering[3]. The refrainment from selves is called the virtue of hiddenness and distance[4].

---

1. Only some residue of a Chinese character remains in Silk Text A. The character cannot be recognized and indicates a different character from the other versions.
2. This statement is repeated in Chapter 58.
3. This statement is repeated in Chapter 58.
4. The virtue of hiddenness and distance is also described in Chapter 29 and Chapter 58. Hiddenness is equivalent to the act of hiding personal interests. Distance means no involvement with objects.

16

There is the inception of all under heaven; that can be the mother of all under heaven. Love[1] gets the Mother by whom one knows her son[2]. After returning to the Mother and keeping her, one has no danger as his/her body is submerged.

1. See Chapter 64 for the discussion of love.
2. Her son refers to all under heaven.

17

As one blocks his/her two mental doors[1] and closes his/her acts of hearing[2], he/she is not bound to earth after death. As one opens his/her worry and achieves his/her enterprises, he/she grows no more after death. The ability to see minuteness is called illumination; the ability to maintain tenderness is called mental strength[3]. An illuminated one uses the Dao's light in his/her daily life. He/she returns to her brightness but does not pursue a long physical life; this is called the inheritance of permanence.

---

1. According to the context, one refers to the mental door for subjectiveness (i.e., being self-opinionated), and the other refers to the mental door for arrogance.
2. Hear: to learn by the ear. See Chapter 21 and Chapter 53 for more information about the closure of hearing.
3. Mental strength is also described in Chapter 20 and Chapter 79.

18

Let me refrain from having knowledge: Walking in the great Dao, I am only afraid of it[1]. The great Dao is very peaceful. However, people tend to deviate from her. They seldom rise in the morning; farmlands are scarcely tended. Barns are scarcely filled; they engage in rhetoric, wear sharp swords, and overeat. They have surplus goods; it is called chimes to invite thieves. The chimes are not the Dao.

---

1. In other words, knowledge causes the separation from the Dao.

19

One who is good at development does not exert regulations; one who is good at holding the Dao does not separate, so descendants will offer sacrifices to him/her endlessly. If one withdraws[1] to develop oneself, then his/her nature will transform and rise to heaven. If a householder withdraws to develop his/her family, then his/her nature will survive. If a village head withdraws to develop his/her village, then his/her nature will last long. If a ruler withdraws to develop his/her state, then his/her nature will be restrained. If a king withdraws to develop his/her kingdom, then his/her nature will be completely open-minded[2]. One should observe oneself, a householder should observe his/her family, a village head should observe his/her village, a ruler should observe his/her state, and a king should observe his/her kingdom[3]. How do I know that the condition of such a kingdom is abundant? By the Incomparable.

---

1. Withdraw: to remove oneself from regulations.
2. Such a king follows the Dao solely (see Chapter 67).
3. Responsible persons need to identify issues in initial stages by observations.

20

One who contains deep virtue[1] is like a baby[2]. He does not get stung by wasps and scorpions as he meets them. He does not get attacked by snatching birds and cruel beasts as he grabs them. He can grasp tightly, although his bone is weak and his tendon is tender. His penis erects although he does not know intercourse between a female and a male; vitality has come. He is no longer emotional after he stops yelling and crying; harmony has come. Harmony calls for the concealment of self-interests[3]; knowing harmony is called illumination. The act of benefiting life calls for tenderness; the heart's ability to control temper is called mental strength[4]. One becomes old once he/she becomes stout[5]. Being stout is called the non-Dao state; a non-Dao one ends early.

---

1. Virtue refers to the Water/Oneness that can be accumulated.
2. Refers to a baby boy.
3. See Chapter 64 for the further discussion of it.
4. The ability to control temper is the same as the ability to maintain tenderness in Chapter 17. Both are the ability to conquer oneself as stated in Chapter 79.
5. Stout: strong in manner like having a bad temper, uncompromising, etc. This and following sentences are repeated in Chapter 76.

21

The knowing one does not talk[1]; a talking one does not know. As one blocks his/her worry, closes his/her acts of hearing, is in harmony with the Dao's light, merges in the dust[2], is not moved by observation[3], and resolves his/her bondages, he/she unifies in the hidden and distant uniformity. Thus, we cannot get the Dao to be either her relatives or estranged from her, neither sharp nor harmed, and neither haughty nor shallow. Hence, the Dao is noble over all under heaven[4].

---

1. The knowing one refers to the Dao.
2. The dust refers to what is produced by the Dao. The phrase means that one becomes small.
3. One is disengaged during the observation.
4. This sentence is repeated in Chapter 27.

22

Develop a state by the standard[1]; use the survival strategy in war[2]; acquire all under heaven by no issues. How do I know if the state of all under heaven is broken? People are poorer as there are more taboos under heaven. States are more disordered as people have more powerful weapons. More burdens arise as people have more knowledge. There are more thieves and murderers as more laws are made. Therefore, a saint says: "As I have nonaction, people are self-evolving. As I like to do inspections, people are self-rectifying[3]. As I do not make trouble, people are self-enriching. As I desire no desire, people embrace the Private Place[4] by themselves."

---

1. According to Chapter 2, the standard is to follow Oneness. This is also the original meaning of standard in Chinese. To follow Oneness, one shall refrain from knowledge (see Chapter 29).
2. See Chapter 36 for illustration.
3. This and previous sentences describe that the saint is open-minded and cautious.
4. Being in the Private Place means the hiddenness of oneself. It also appears in Chapters 63, 65, 74, 75, 78, and 83.

23

The more controls a ruler implements, the more difficulties his/her state faces. The more inspections a ruler engages in, the more expansive his/her state is. Calamity leans to luckiness; luckiness hides calamity. People who know their limits of tolerance do not have the act of following Oneness; it is instead viewed as oddness; kindness is instead viewed as harm. Human astray has been stubborn for a long time. Therefore, one should not divide but rather unite, not mock but rather be tolerant, not control but rather let go, and not skew[1] but rather be luminous.

---

1. Skew: look obliquely to show disdain.

24

For managing people and serving heaven, nothing is on par with caution. Only because of caution, one works early[1]. The early work is called the heavy accumulation of virtue[2]. Nothing cannot be shouldered[3] due to the heavy accumulation of virtue. If nothing cannot be shouldered, one's limit cannot be known. If one's limit cannot be known, he/she can have a country. Having the mother of countries[4], one can be eternal. It is called the deep reach to the solid base, i.e., the long-lived Dao with the lasting watch.

---

1. See Chapters 28 and 29 for the discussion of caution and the early work.
2. See Chapter 14 for the importance of virtue.
3. Shoulder: undertake responsibility.
4. The mother of countries refers to the Dao according to the context.

25

A saint managing a big country behaves like enjoying a small delicious fish[1]. As the Dao is under heaven, ghosts are not magical. It is not that ghosts are not magical, but that gods do not harm people. Not only do gods not harm people, but the saint also corrects people's harmful acts. Gods and people do not harm each other[2], so virtue crosses and returns.

1. We need to be careful to remove fish bones.
2. Natural events, e.g., rain, wind, flood, etc., are controlled by gods in the traditional Chinese culture. In modern words, people live in harmony with nature.

26

A big state is downstream. It is a female state of the kingdom and an approximation of the kingdom. Females always prevail over males by their attraction. For their attraction, being in a lower position is suitable. If a big state places itself in a lower position than a small state, then it will acquire the small state. If a small state places itself lower than a big state, then it will be acquired. Thus, either acquisition or being acquired is due to being in a lower position. Hence, a big state only wants to merge livestock and people; a small state only wants to join and serve people. Both are satisfied. Hence, a big state should be in a lower position.

27

The Dao is a pour[1] in all objects. She is the protector of mild people, while unkind people seek her protection. Beautiful words can advertise; admiring acts can give pleasure[2]. About unkind people, burden makes them abandon their possessions. Hence, an administration is set up with the son of heaven[3] and governing rules. Although unkind people have four-horse vehicles with round flat pieces of jade in the front to show their nobility, they sit and enter the Incomparable[4]. Why was this being esteemed in ancient times? Does it say: "Seek to get the Dao, and so sins are pardoned from carrying."? Hence, the Dao is noble over all under heaven.

---

1. The Dao is called the God of Creek in Chapter 54.
2. Beautiful words and admiring acts are not mild.
3. In ancient China, the emperors were called the son of heaven to show their supreme power was given by heaven.
4. See Chapter 21 about how to enter the Dao.

28

Act for nonaction[1]. Resolve issues for no issues. Taste[2] for the tasteless[3]; treat small things as big things, and few things as many things; respond to enmity with kindness. If one considers difficulties ahead, then things become easy. If one acts for great things, then they turn out to be small. Difficulties under heaven arise from ease; greatness under heaven arises from smallness[4]. Therefore, saints never act for greatness and then become great[5]. One who consents easily has little trust for certain; one who thinks how easy things are has a lot of trouble for certain. Therefore, saints are hesitant[6] and take things seriously. Thus, they end up in no trouble.

---

1. Acting for nonaction is the process of reducing intended actions (see Chapter 11).
2. Taste: perceive of something, however limited or slight.
3. The tasteless refers to words from the Dao (see Chapter 81).
4. It refers to smallness on the mental level, which means carefulness in Chinese. Because of carefulness, he/she can discern minuteness. The ability to see minuteness is called illumination (see Chapter 17).
5. A similar statement in Chapter 80.
6. Hesitant: slow to say under uncertainty.

29

It is easy to maintain when it is stable; it is easy to plan when it is not cracked. It is easy to break when it is fragile; it is easy to disperse when it is hidden. Act for it before it comes into being; manage it before it is disorderly. Wood that is so large to be embraced by several persons arises from tininess; a grand platform that goes through nine-time completion arises from weak soil; highness of hundreds of benevolences takes pleasure in lowness. Actions for great things damage them; holding things loses them. Therefore, a saint has no actions for purposes and thus no destructions; he/she has no holding and thus no loss. For people's enterprises, they will always be ruined after achievements. Thus, if we are vigilant after achievements as we do in beginnings, then there are no destructions. Therefore, a saint desires no desire and so does not value rare goods; he/she learns not to be learned[1] and so returns people from their excessiveness; he/she can assist all subjects to be themselves and so corrects

---

1. The state of not being learned is refrainment from knowledge according to the context.

their aggressive actions. Hence, it states: "For the Dao, a ruler shall not enlighten people but rather stupefy them. It is difficult to manage people in that they have knowledge. Thus, if a ruler knows the state by knowledge, it grows evildoers; if a ruler knows the state without knowledge[2], it grows virtue. Always knowing these two facts, a ruler is in the mode of restraint[3]. With knowing the mode of restraint always, the refrainment is called the virtue of hiddenness and distance. The virtue of hiddenness and distance is deep, distant, and opposite to being an object. Then, the ruler reaches greatness and smoothness."

---

2. Without knowledge, one knows by the Dao (see Chapter 37).
3. Restraint: the act of restraining, holding back, controlling, or checking.

30

Rivers and seas are kings of hundreds of creeks in that they are good at placing themselves lower than creeks. Therefore, they can be the kings of hundreds of creeks. Therefore, desiring to be above people, a saint certainly use humble language to put himself/herself lower than people. Desiring to be ahead, he/she certainly put himself/herself behind people. So, the saint stays ahead, but people do not harm him/her; he/she stays above, but people do not feel pressured. All under heaven like to gather around him/her and do not loathe him/her. Isn't it because the saint has no persuasion? So, all under heaven cannot compete with him/her.

31

A state should be small with few people in it. Let a tool of tens or hundreds of people not be used; let people take death seriously by exile. There are vehicles but no places around to ride them; there are armors and weapons but no chances to display them. Let people return to using knotted strings[1] instead of the written language for recording. They enjoy their delicious food, rejoice in their works, take pleasure in their customs, and reside in peace. Adjacent states watch each other, sounds of chickens and dogs can be heard mutually, and people do not contact mutually until they die of old age.

---

1. Before the invention of the written language, knotted strings were used to record information in several cultures, like the Chinese and the Incas.

32

Trustworthy words are not beautiful; beautiful words are trustless. Knowledgeable people do not have broad knowledge; people with broad knowledge are not knowledgeable. Mild people do not accumulate a lot; people who accumulate a lot are unkind.

33

Saints have no accumulation. By using their knowledge for people, they empty the possessions; by giving what they have a lot to people, they unload the massiveness. Hence, the heavenly Dao is beneficial but not harmful; to do but not compete should be the human way.

34

All under heaven[1] say: "I am great and have no darkness." No darkness is solely due to greatness. If one has darkness, he/she has been small for a long time. I have three suggestions to preserve greatness always. First is tenderness; second is inspection; third is no act of competing for the forefront under heaven. Because of tenderness, one can be expressive. Because of inspection, one can have broad potential. Because of no act of competing for the forefront under heaven, one can be the head of achievements. Now, if one abandons tenderness and is expressive, and he/she abandons the back and is aggressive, then he/she will get killed for certain. Because of tenderness, one can win in fights and be firm in defense. Heaven will establish a person if the Woman surrounds him/her with tenderness[2].

---

1. It refers to the Dao's kingdom that consists of pure light (see Chapter 17).
2. The Woman refers to the Dao; heaven abides by her (see Chapter 71).

35

One who is good at being an intelligent person does not use force. One who is good at fighting does not get angry. One who is good at defeating enemies does not associate. One who is good at employing people puts oneself lower than them. This is called the virtue of no dissuasion; this is called people's empowerment; this is called the limit of heaven and ancient times.

36

There is a proverb about war strategies: "I dare not to be a host but rather a guest. I do not want to advance an inch but rather belittle my army by retreating several feet." This is called nowhere to go, no arms to raise, and no weapon to hold. Then, it is invincible. There is no darker misfortune than no consolation. No consolation cuts me down deadly, and I defend fully. Therefore, if two armies are about the same strength, a grieved one defeats the other.

37

My words are easy to understand and follow. However, people cannot understand them, so they cannot follow them. Speech has the ruler[1]; issues have ancestors[2]. Only because of no knowledge, one is not self-opinionated. Knowing people are few, so I[3] am precious. Therefore, saints appear to be dusky but hold the gem within[4].

---

1. We are the ruler of our speech and so can control it.
2. Issues have root causes.
3. The pronoun 'I' refers to the Dao. According to the context, one who knows by knowledge is self-opinionated; one who knows by the Dao is all-knowing. Knowledge is Dao's flowers but not the Dao herself (see Chapter 1), and knowledge is the reason for a person to separate from the Dao (see Chapter 18).
4. The gem within refers to the Dao.

38

One who knows not to know by knowledge is long-lived[1]; one who does not know not to know by knowledge is sick. Therefore, saints are not sick in that they are sick of the sickness. Therefore, they are not sick.

---

1. The act of not knowing by knowledge is equivalent to the act of not being self-opinionated (see the previous chapter for the background). So, the act of not knowing by knowledge is an act of not being full (see Chapter 40); one with no acts of being full can be old without being finished (see Chapter 63).

39

If people do not fear fearful things, then big fearful things will come soon.

40

The Mother[1] closes and opens her abode; she does not dislike what she bears. Only if one is not full[2], then he/she is not repellent[3]. Therefore, saints are self-aware but not self-opinionated; they are self-respecting but not arrogant. Hence, we shall remove the cover to get the Incomparable.

---

1. Here, the Mother refers to the Dao.
2. The act of not being full means the act of not being self-opinionated and the act of not being arrogant by noticing the logical connector 'therefore'.
3. See Chapter 68 for the discussion from the opposite perspective.

41

People who dare to be aggressive[1] need to be killed; people who have the courage not to be aggressive survive. For these two types, one is beneficial, and the other is harmful. About what heaven dislikes, the reason is well-known, i.e., because of the Dao of heaven. She does not attack but is good at winning; she does not speak but is good at response; she does not need to be summoned but comes by herself. She is quick in actions and good at strategizing. The heavenly net touches all objects, sparse but not missing.

---

1. Aggressive people have ambitions according to Chapter 79.

42

If people are obstinate and do not fear death, what should we do? Kill to make them fear. If the obstinacy means death, then I find out such people and kill them. Who dares! If people are obstinate and certainly fear death, then there are executioners always[1]. Showing off executioners' killing is like showing off great carpenters' chopping. Showing off their chopping, great carpenters seldom do not hurt their hands.

---

1. This sentence implies that the obstinacy is the cause of crimes.

43

People have a bad harvest in that they acquire excessive food resources. Hence, they have a bad harvest[1]. People are unmanageable in that their ruler acts by knowledge. Thus, they are unmanageable.

---

1. For example, overfishing causes fish to become depleted or underpopulated.

44

People weave death in that they pursue a luxurious life. Therefore, they weave death. Only if one does not do for a living, then wealth and nobility come.

45

When people are born, they are soft and feeble; when they die, they are solid, big, wealthy, and strong. When all animals, grasses, and woods begin their life, they are soft and fragile; their deaths create pillars and feasts. So, it says: "Solidness and strength are death[1]; softness, weakness, hiddenness, and smallness are life." If an army is strong, it cannot win. If wood is strong, it becomes a lasting pillar. Strength is inferior; softness, weakness, hiddenness, and smallness are superior.

---

1 In contrast, the mental strength described in Chapter 17, Chapter 20, and Chapter 79 is praised.

46

The Dao under heaven resembles one who is drawing a bow[1]. As a high one let her rule, subjects support her. Ones with surpluses reduce her presence; ones in deficiency are supplied with her presence. Hence, the heavenly Dao reduces surpluses and benefits deficiencies. But, the human way does not. It deteriorates deficiencies to offer to surpluses. Who can offer possessions to the heavenly one if they have surpluses? Only those who have the Dao. Therefore, saints do but do not have possession; they succeed but do not dwell on achievements[2]. One without such desires sees wealth.

---

1. The Dao is ready and quick in actions (see Chapter 41 as well).
2. This sentence is repeated in Chapter 50.

47

Nothing under heaven is more tender than the Water, but attacking, solid, and strong ones cannot be ahead of it since the Water does not react against them. The Water defeats rigidity; weakness defeats strength. Since people under heaven do not correct their knowledge, they cannot follow them. Hence, the saint's words state: "One who bears the state's humiliation is called the chief of gods of lands and grains; one who bears the state's hostility is called the king of all under heaven." The right words seem the opposite.

48

Though one reconciles a big resentment, there must be a residual resentment. How can he/she be benign? Therefore, a saint blesses refrainment and so does not blame people. Hence, one with virtue exerts refrainment; one without virtue exerts throws. The heavenly Dao has no intimates and is always with a gentle one.

PART II:

CANON OF DAO (DAO JING)

49

Sayable principles are not permanent principles; namable names are not permanent names. The unnamable is the start of all objects; having names is the mother of all objects[1]. Hence, one who always has no desire observes invisibles; one who always has desires observes those being called[2]. These two things[3] come from the uniformity but have different names. The uniformity is called the hidden distance in the hidden distance, the door of countless invisibles.

---

1. This statement is similar to the sentence in Chapter 4—objects under heaven are born from possessions.
2. He/she is imprisoned by those being called.
3. These two things refer to invisibles and those being called.

✿✿✿✿✿✿✿ **50** ✿✿✿✿✿✿✿

If all in a kingdom know goodness and behave for
goodness, then evil stops. All know kindness corrects unkindness, and that is it. The appearance
of deficiency starts with possessions[1]; the appearance of ease completes the cautious attitude[2]; the
appearance of brevity impedes actions for longevity[3]; the appearance of lowness fulfills actions for
highness[4]; tones reflect meanings; the appearance
of falling behind falls with actions for being ahead[5];
these statements are always true. Therefore, a
king as a Dao's messenger[6] dwells on the post of
nonaction and implements nonverbal guidance;
all objects are at peace but do not start[7], act but
do not set expectations, and succeed but do not

---

1. Holding things loses them (see Chapter 29). Meanwhile, if one is totally
   free of possessions, he/she has all under heaven.
2. Meanwhile, difficulties under heaven arise from the attitude of ease (see
   Chapter 28).
3. Meanwhile, one who does not live for oneself has a long life (see
   Chapter 55).
4. Meanwhile, a humble person will achieve a high social rank. See Chapter
   2 and Chapter 30 for illustration.
5. Meanwhile, a saint put themself behind to be ahead (see Chapter 30).
6. A Dao's messenger is a person who connects to the Dao and follows the
   Dao solely. A Dao's messenger is called a saint in the Canon of Virtue.
7. See Chapter 83 for the details.

dwell on achievements. Only if a king ceases from motion, thereby discordance in his/her kingdom is corrected.

51

Do not offer fortunes for people not to compete; do not value rare goods for people not to be thieves; do not expose desirable things for people not to be disturbed. Therefore, the management of a king as a Dao's messenger is to empty their hearts, fill their bellies, weaken their wills, and strengthen their bones. Let people have no knowledge and no desire always. Let people know not to be aggressive[1], so they correct their actions to stop aggression. Then, nothing cannot be managed[2].

---

1. This is consistent with Chapter 41.
2. In other words, everything can be managed.

52

The Dao streams. What she streams is not full for use; it is so deep and clear that the ancestors of all objects start there. I stabilize[1] in meditation, resolve my bondages, harmonize with the Dao's light, and merge in the dust[2]. As I submerge, some object[3] starts to exist. I do not know whose descendant she is. She exists before the imperial image[4].

---

1. It is similar to 'not moved by observation' in Chapter 21.
2. The last three clauses appear in Chapter 21 in the different order.
3. Some object refers to the Dao.
4. The imperial image refers to what the Dao streams. It can manage all under heaven for the best results (see Chapter 81).

53

Heaven and earth are not benevolent in that they take all objects to be sheepdogs[1]. Dao's messengers are not benevolent in that they take hundreds of introspections to be the sheepdog[2]. Between heaven and earth, Dao's messengers carry the key[3] within the cloth. As they reach the emptiness, they do not disturb it. Then, the Dao streams as they follow her. The more we hear, the more limited our minds are. Then, we would rather hold the inner one.

---

1. Sheepdog: a dog used to tend, guard, or drive sheep. This sentence describes that heaven and earth make all objects under heaven mutually watch. Thus, heaven and earth are not benevolent.
2. This sentence describes that Dao's messengers do not have their prejudices but follow the Dao who is the supreme guide after hundreds of introspections.
3. The key refers to the Dao since only the Dao is good at initiation and accomplishment (see Chapter 3).

54

The God of the Creek[1] never dies. It is called the hidden and distant female. The door of the hidden and distant female is called the root of heaven and earth. The Creek is so subtle that it seems to exist indefinitely. Its use is unexhausted.

---

1. The God of the Creek refers to the Dao.

55

Heaven is long; earth is lasting. Heaven and earth are long and lasting in that they do not live for themselves. Hence, they are long-lived. Therefore, Dao's messengers keep themselves gentle and small and so are ahead; they place themselves aside and so survive. Isn't it because they have no selfishness to carry? Hence, their selves[1] get fulfilled.

---

1. Selves: personal interests.

56 [1]

Upper kindness administers the Water[2]. The Water is good at benefiting all objects and has the act of inspecting; it stays in the places that are disliked by the multitude. Hence, it is almost identical to the Dao. The Water is good at being down-to-earth for residence, good at making hearts deep and clear, good at being trustworthy for an offer, good at management for government, good at accomplishing work, and good at selecting proper moments for service. Only because of no inspection, one is not excellent.

---

1. This chapter provides a background for obtaining Oneness and being lowly in Chapter 2.
2. The Water is another name for what is produced by the Dao and is also called the Dao's Words or Oneness.

57

It is better to stop than to increase wealth/fame on crutches[1]. [...][2], [...][3] can keep them[4] for a long time. Having a full room of gold and gems, we cannot keep them long. Being proud of nobility and richness, we leave ourselves disasters. After achievements are narrated, keeping ourselves gentle and small is the divine law[5].

---

1. People often sacrifice themselves to pursue wealth/fame, but what is their use if we do not have a life? See Chapter 61 for the general discussion.
2. There are six Chinese characters in Silk Text A, while four characters in other versions. Furthermore, Silk Text A alone cannot determine the meaning of the clause due to four missing characters. Thus, the translation is averted.
3. Only some residue of a character remains in Silk Text A. The character seems to be the word evil, while it is the word no in the other versions.
4. What the pronoun refers to cannot be determined due to the unknown clause.
5. Without dwelling on achievements, one can be open and keep moving forward, while one ends early if he/she dwells on achievements to be strong (see Chapter 76).

58

Residing in a physical body to embrace Oneness, can one not be separated from Oneness? Smoothing the breath to reach softness[1], can one be a baby? Repairing and removing hidden and distant blue[2], can one have no defects? Loving people and making a state survive, can a ruler do them without depending on knowledge? Can the one who opens and closes the door of heaven be female[3]? Can one be all-knowing without depending on knowledge[4]? The Dao bears us and raises us. She gives birth but does not have the act of owning; she promotes growth but does not have the act of slaughtering. The refrainment is called the virtue of hiddenness and distance.

---

1. One who reaches softness has freedom (see Chapter 6).
2. Hidden and distant blue refers to darkness in Chapter 4.
3. See the answer in Chapter 40.
4. See the answer in Chapter 37.

59

Thirty spokes are put into a hub of a wheel; a cart is useful because of its space. Clay is fired to make a vessel; a vessel is useful because of its space. Doors and windows are dug; a room is useful because of its space. So, possession[1] makes a person sharp; emptying one's possessions makes him/her useful[2].

---

1. Possession: the act of possessing.
2. This statement is consistent with the sentence in Chapter 3—the virtue of creativity follows from emptying.

60

Five colors make people's eyes bright; solemn parades[1] make people crazy; rare goods make people travel together; five flavors make people gorge; five tones make people deaf[2]. Therefore, the management of a king as a Dao's messenger is for bellies but not for eyes[3]. Hence, remove the trapping nets to hear the Incomparable.

---

1. For example, military parades.
2. Five tones make people deaf to supreme sound from the Dao since supreme sound is almost inaudible (see Chapter 3).
3. Because of bright eyes, people look for desirable things. The bright eyes are the first to cause desires.

61 [1]

Reputation and disgrace are disturbing; one values large goods as oneself. A disease[2] is said to the disturbing mind caused by reputation and disgrace. Reputation is inferior in that people get disturbed by obtaining it and by losing it as well. Thus, it says that reputation and disgrace are disturbing. One who values large goods as oneself is burdened. I have large goods in that I have this life. If I do not have this life, what goods can I have? Hence, if one regards that preserving his/her life is more important than serving all under heaven, then such a person can be entrusted with all under heaven. If one likes to sacrifice oneself to serve all under heaven, what can the Woman[3] use to entrust all under heaven?

---

1. This chapter is related to Chapter 7.
2. The word 'disease' consists of the prefix 'dis' and the word 'ease'. Hence, a disease comes for the disturbing mind.
3. The Woman refers to the Dao.

62

I look at it[1] but cannot see it, and then it is called a faint sound[2]. I listen to it but cannot hear it, and then it is called sparseness[3]. I touch it but cannot get it, and then it is called levelness[4]. These three cannot be reached for identification. Thus, they are mixed into Oneness. For Oneness, its top is not tightened; its bottom does not disappear. As I reason about it, it is unnamable and then at once returns to nothing[5]. It is called the non-state state and the image without an object. It is called a return to the origin by ignorance. I follow it but cannot see where its back ends; I face it but cannot see where its head starts. Holding the present Dao, one drives current possessions to know ancient beginning. It is called the restraining power of the Dao.

---

1. The pronoun refers to Oneness that is produced by the Dao.
2. When the mind focuses on looking, it becomes faint sounds.
3. When the mind focuses on listening, it becomes dust.
4. When the mind focuses on touching, it becomes level.
5. Reasoning causes the disappearance of Oneness.

63

For the Dao, ancient immortals are hidden and small and reach the hidden distance. They are too profound to be described. Because they are indescribable, I forcibly sketch them: They associate like wading in winter; they hesitate like fearing neighbors; they are solemn like guests; they are dispersive like water moistening[1]; they [...][2] as they choose the Private Place; they are unfathomable as they choose to be muddy[3]; they are unfettered as they choose to cleanse themselves. Lucidness comes by reaching love[4] to clear turbidity; life comes by esteeming the Woman[5]. They cherish this Dao but do not desire to be full[6]. Only because of no desire to be full, they can be old without being finished.

---

1. They are supportive but not demanding.
2. Here, only the left part of a Chinese character remains in Silk Text A. It indicates a different character from the other versions.
3. In other words, they keep a low profile.
4. See the next chapter for how to reach love.
5. The Woman refers to the Dao.
6. See Chapter 40 for the explanation of the act of not being full.

64

Guard against sentiments after reaching the summit of emptiness[1]. Then, myriad objects arise around. I observe their return: Heaven and objects become cloudy and return to their root[2]. It is called love[3]. Love is called the return from demand. As one returns from demand, he/she conceals self-interests. One who knows the concealment is illuminated or blind otherwise; blind acts are disturbing. Tolerance follows the state of knowing the concealment of self-interests; justice follows tolerance; being a king follows justice; the acquisition of all under heaven follows the state of being a king; having the Dao follows the acquisition; eternity follows the state of having the Dao. As one's body is submerged, he/she is not a slave of the heart[4].

---

1. It is the state of deep meditation in which the emptiness is not disturbed by the mood (see Chapter 53 as well).
2. Their root is the door of the hidden and distant female (i.e., the Dao) according to Chapter 54.
3. Love follows a clear heart, i.e., possessions are removed.
4. As one is not a slave of the heart, he/she has no dangers (see Chapter 16).

65

For the great highness[1], subjects just know her existence. Next, subjects admire and praise their ruler. Next, subjects fear their ruler. At the bottom, subjects parent their ruler. There are doubts because of inadequate trust. A Dao's messenger is hesitant like treasuring out-of-mouth words[2]. After success and achievement, he/she after hundreds of introspections[3] says: "I am myself." Therefore, as the great Dao is abandoned, there are benevolence and righteousness[4]; as knowledge comes out pleasingly, there are major errors; as family relationships are discordant, there is compliant tenderness; as states are in disorder, there are faithful officials. If verbal guidance and knowledge are abandoned, the sharpness of people is reduced a hundred times; if benevolence and righteousness are abandoned, people return from compliant tenderness; if cleverness and sharpness are abandoned, there

1. The great highness refers to a king as a Dao's messenger since the Dao is the best in managing all under heaven (see, for example, Chapter 78).
2. A Dao's messenger is careful of what he/she says.
3. After hundreds of introspections, he/she has the Dao within (see Chapter 12 and Chapter 53).
4. See Chapter 1 for the definitions of benevolence and righteousness.

are no thieves and robbers. It is not enough to say the above three cases. Thus, let people behave as follows: seeing plain things, embracing the Private Place, being little selfish, having few desires, stopping education, and no worry.

66

How is it different between quick nods and verbal abuses? How does one choose between goodness and hostility? Does one have to fear what people dislike? Look, he/she does not hold the inner one. People are elated as if they tour platforms in spring, though they dwell in the big prison[1]. I rest and am not cheerful, like a quiet baby; the acquisition of essences follows no places to return to[2]. People have surpluses; I alone give out what I have. The hearts of my fellow people are in chaos. Peddlers[3] have a bright appearance; I alone choose to be dusky. Peddlers are in exile; I alone am inclined to be quiet and rest my heart. As I forget myself, those[4] resemble a sea. Look, those seem to stop nowhere. People depend on possessions; I alone listen to the origin to be good-humored. My desire is different from others as I cherish the Mother as my livelihood.

---

1. They are bound on earth.
2. Essences follow the state of standing alone (see Chapter 2 and Chapter 53).
3. Peddlers refer to fellow people according to the previous sentence.
4. Those refer to all under heaven. This and the next sentences signify that all under heaven are vast and ever-changing.

67

The appearance of the nature of complete open-mindedness is to follow the Dao solely. About substances of the Dao, they are observable only by return to the origin and ignorance. By ignorance and return to the origin, there are images inside. As I watch and forget myself, there is some object inside. As I float and sigh, there are invitations inside. The invitations are sincere. Then, there is trust inside. From today to ancient times, her name never leaves to soothe various human authorities[1]. How do I know the states of the human authorities? By the Incomparable.

---

1. See Chapter 2 for the examples of human authorities.

68[1]

A cooking[2] one cannot stand; self's watch is not thorough[3]; a self-opinionated one is not illuminated; a boastful one has no credits; a self-defensive[4] one cannot grow. These behaviors for the Dao are called excessive food and redundant acts. Some objects may dislike them. Hence, a desirous one should not live with them[5].

1. This chapter and Chapter 40 discuss the same topic from the opposite perspective, i.e., being full and not being full.
2. Cook: process by combining ingredients.
3. Self's watch refers to the act of looking with prejudices. The sentence indicates information from self's watch is partial and even deceptive sometimes.
4. Self-defensive: devoted to defending oneself, possessions, ideas, etc.
5. Otherwise, his/her desires will not get fulfilled. See also the next chapter for clarification.

69

One with devious experience will get gold; one who experiences injustice will become calm; one in the valley[1] will become full; something worn-out will be renewed; one who asks for few will be fulfilled; one who acquires a lot will be confused. Thus, a Dao's messenger holds Oneness to shepherd all under heaven. He/she is not self-watching and then is illuminated; he/she is not self-opinionated and then has complete knowledge; he/she does not boast and then has credits; he/she is not self-defensive and then can grow. Only because a Dao's messenger has no verbal guidance, no one else can compete with him/her. Is the ancient proverb, i.e., one with devious experience will get gold, trivial? Indeed, gold will be rewarded to such a person.

---

1. Valley: a gloomy situation or period.

70

Reticence is the state of being oneself. A whirlwind does not last all morning; a storm does not last an entire day. Who makes them? Heaven and earth. But they cannot be eternal. Let alone people. So, the ones who follow and serve the Dao are identical to the Dao; virtuous ones have virtue[1] in common; talkative ones converge into loss. For the ones who have the virtue of sameness, the Dao favors them as well[2]. For the ones who converge into the loss, the Dao loses them too.

---

1. See Chapter 1 for the discussion of virtue. Virtuous ones may have different admirable qualities, but they have a common point as said.
2. A similar statement in Chapter 3—pleasing the Dao follows from similarity.

71

There is an object who has a homogeneous completion; she exists before the creation of heaven and
earth; she is gorgeous and touching; she stands
alone and has no boundary; she can be the mother of
heaven and earth. I do not know her name and call
her by the word—Dao. I name her forcibly and call
her greatness. Greatness calls for prophecy; prophecy calls for distance; distance calls for refrainment.
The Dao is great; heaven is great; earth is great; a
king is also great. So, there are four authorities in a
country; the king is one of them. Human laws are
limited by earth; earth's laws are limited by heaven;
heaven's laws are limited by the Dao; the Dao's laws
are only limited by herself.

72

Caution is the root of the hidden Water; lucid-ness[1] dominates haste. Therefore, a respectful man does not leave his attention from accidents and important things during his journey. Only if an overseeing official is hidden and distant, he/she is lucid. However, a king veiled by tens of thousands of coverings[2] manages all under heaven personally. Base is lost due to the management; the supremacy is lost due to haste.

---

1. Lucidness: the state of clear understanding.
2. He/she is veiled by bias due to his/her possessions.

73

One who is good at travel does not leave a trace; one who is good at speaking does not produce defective comfort; one who is good at calculation does not use an abacus; one is so good at locking a door that it cannot be opened without the key; one is so good at tying a knot that it cannot be freed without knowing the tying arrangement. Therefore, Dao's messengers are always good at encouraging people, so there are no abandoned people. Objects do not abandon their talents; this is called illumination through the restrained heart. Thus, mild people are teachers for benign people; unkind people are gifts for benign people. If we do not value the teachers and love the gifts, we only have the knowledge but close our eyes tightly. It is called the blind point.

ꙮꙮꙮ 74[1] ꙮꙮꙮ

Knowing oneself strong but keeping oneself gentle, one is tolerant for all under heaven. As one is tolerant for all under heaven, his/her permanent nature is not excitable. If he/she is always not excitable, then he/she returns to a baby. Knowing oneself innocent but keeping that disgrace, one bathes for all under heaven. As one bathes for all under heaven, his/her permanent nature is lowly. If his/her nature is lowly, then he/she returns to the Private Place. Knowing oneself and keeping oneself hidden[2], one leads for all under heaven. As one leads for all under heaven, his/her permanent nature does not follow others to pursue goods. If his/her nature does not follow others to pursue goods, then he/she returns to the unlimited state.

---

1. The chapter is the continuation of the previous chapter to discuss how to restrain the heart.
2. See Chapter 82 for clarification.

⁂ 75 ⁂

One becomes an instrument after the Private Place scatters. A Dao's messenger uses it[1] and so is the head of officers. The great regulation[2] does not divide people. One acts to acquire all under heaven, but I do not see that he/she will get it to stop. All-under-heaven is a divine instrument, not an object for actions. One who acts for it[3] will damage it; one who holds it will lose it. Some objects travel; some follow; some are bright; some are dull; some are in company; some are fallen; some are wicked; some are abandoned. Therefore, a Dao's messenger removes overindulgence, big things, and stationery.

---

1. The pronoun 'it' refers to the Private Place.
2. It refers to the regulation from the Dao. See Chapter 78 and Chapter 83 for the details.
3. The pronoun 'it' refers to the acquisition of all under heaven.

76

A ruler assisted by the Dao does not use military forces to be strong in front of all under heaven. Military action is easy to get retaliated; the place where an army stays is grown with thistles and thorns. A mild one attains[1] and stops; he/she does not attain to be formidable. The following things are called the state of not being strong by attainment: Do not be arrogant by attainment; do not be defensive by attainment; do not harm after attainment[2]; do not stop and dwell on it after attainment. One becomes old once he/she becomes stout. Being stout is called the non-Dao state; a non-Dao one ends early.

---

1. Attain: to succeed in obtaining something.
2. For example, do not kill surrendered soldiers.

77

An army is a lethal instrument. Some objects may dislike it. Hence, a desirous ruler[1] should not live with it. Respectful men value assistance in daily life; blessing[2] is valued as an army is used. Thus, an army is not an instrument for respectful men. An army is a lethal instrument; it is used as the last resort; sharp raids are superior strategies. Do not praise military attacks. If a ruler praises them, he/she enjoys carnage. A ruler who enjoys carnage cannot succeed in acquiring all under heaven. Therefore, assistance is offered for happy events; blessing is offered for funeral services. Therefore, pacifying generals should dwell on assistance; the upper general should dwell on blessing, i.e., his/her style of speaking should comply with funeral manners. If the military slays many, they should stand with sorrow to mourn it; if the military triumphs, they should hold funeral ceremonies to treat it.

---

1. A desirous ruler refers to a ruler who desires to acquire all under heaven.
2. Blessing: the invoking of divine favor by particular behaviors. According to the chapter, the particular behaviors refer to the compliance with funeral manners.

78

The Dao is always unnamable; the Private Place quickly responds to smallness, so aggressiveness and submission under heaven are corrected[1]. If a king can keep the Dao, then all subjects will become guest-like[2] by themselves; heaven and earth together are like a valley to convey the sweet Water[3]; people do not need to be ordered and share within themselves. The beginning rules have names. If there are names already, then we need to know refrainment. One with the awareness of refrainment has no dangers. As the servant Dao[4] is under heaven[5], she is like a small creek flowing to a river/sea.

---

1. See Chapter 83 for clarification.
2. Guest-like: resembling a guest. Characteristics of guests are alertness, self-restraint, and so on.
3. The sweet Water refers to what the Dao streams, and it is also called outgoing words from the Dao (see Chapter 81).
4. The Dao provides a lot of great things (see Chapter 81 as well) if a king can hold the Dao. So, the Dao is called the servant here.
5. The other stipulation is that the Dao is not under heaven (see Chapter 9).

79

One who knows others has knowledge[1]; one who knows oneself is illuminated. One who conquers others has strength; one who conquers oneself is mentally strong[2]. One who knows to be lowly is rich; one who forces to move has ambitions. One who does not lose that abode has a long life[3]; one who does not forget after death[4] is lasting.

---

1. Judging others by knowledge is not recommended since dependence on knowledge is depreciated (see Chapter 38).
2. In other words, one can control his/her temper (see Chapter 20), or one has the ability to maintain tenderness (see Chapter 17).
3. See Chapter 40 for how not to lose the abode.
4. See Chapter 17 for how to achieve it.

80

The Dao let objects be and can aid and bless. After completion and achievement, she does not claim possession. Myriad objects return to her, but she does not want to be the monarch. Then, she always has no desire and can be named as triviality. Myriad objects return to her, but she does not want to be the monarch. She can be named the great. Therefore, Dao's messengers become great in that they do not act for greatness. Therefore, they become great.

81

As a king holds the great image, all under heaven gather. There is no harm in the gathering. Instead, it is safe, peaceful, and great for all under heaven. She likes to give food and stops excesses. So, about words outgoing from the Dao, it states: "Her talk is tasteless. As we look, they are not enough to be seen. As we listen, they are not enough to be heard. As we use them, they are endless."

82

If one wants to harvest that[1], then he/she must expand that; if one wants to weaken that, then he/she must strengthen that; if one wants to remove that, then he/she must associate with that; if one wants to seize from that, then he/she must give to that. It is called illumination from hiddenness. Weakness, along with friendliness, is better than strength. Fish is not separate from the deep and clear Water[2]; powerful weapons of a state cannot be shown to people.

---

1. That: an object as supposed to be understood.
2. Therefore, trust in the Dao (see Chapter 41 for illustration) and remain gentle.

83

The Dao is always unnamable. If a king can keep her, all subjects will make their hearts. As they make their hearts and desire to rise, I will fulfill them in the unnamable Private Place. Being fulfilled in the unnamable Private Place, they will not be disgraced. As they are not disgraced, they will have love. Then, heaven and earth will be self-rectifying.

Acknowledgments

My deep appreciation goes to you, the reader, for sharing the message with your family and friends from love. With your help, the message of the truth will spread to the world. May you be favored by the Dao. The book will benefit your loved ones for the better life as well.

I express my gratitude to three professionals for contributing to the formation of the second edition: Hannah Gaskamp for the creative cover design, Sandra Jurca for the interior design and layout, and EM Kinga Mac for line editing for a more concise text. All remaining errors are my own. If you have any suggestions or corrections, please let me know. Your kindness is greatly appreciated.

My special thanks to Laozi for writing Dao De Jing. It is my great fortune to have a chance to read this invaluable book. Last but not least, I am deeply grateful to the Dao. Without guidance from her, I could never understand this great book and then find the direction of my life.

About the Translator

Dr. Jinchun Ye is a Chinese-born U.S. resident. He received his education in China until master's studies. Later, he went to the United States for further studies and earned his Ph.D. degree in applied Math. As a quantitative researcher, he has published a dozen research papers in academic journals and conferences, including two single-authored papers in a prestigious journal. Dr. Ye is always fascinated by Dao De Jing. He has been immersed in studying it for many years. With curiosity and hard work, he deciphered Dao De Jing to reveal the hidden way to success, freedom, and eternity.

About the Translator